Contents

Page

3   About this devotional booklet

Week 1 – Family

7   **Day 1**   Church is called to be family
9   **Day 2**   A family knows me and needs me to contribute
11   **Day 3**   Healthy church family is a powerful witness
13   **Day 4**   Mission is meant to be done together as family
15   **Day 5**   The people in our world need a real family
17   Survey 1

Week 2 – Place

21   **Day 1**   God has a purpose for our church family being where it is
23   **Day 2**   Embracing our place
25   **Day 3**   Growing local relationships
27   **Day 4**   Restoring our place
29   **Day 5**   Persevering for the sake of our place
31   Survey 2

Week 3 – Mission

35   **Day 1**   Your relationships are your church's mission
37   **Day 2**   Your mission is a perfect fit for you
39   **Day 3**   Beginning a redemptive relationship
41   **Day 4**   Spiritual conversations
43   **Day 5**   What about those I cannot connect to my church family?
45   Survey 3

Contents

Week 4 – Together

49	Day 1	Doing mission together as family
51	Day 2	Bringing my two worlds together
53	Day 3	Serving together in our place
55	Day 4	The role of church programmes
57	Day 5	A place for others at the family table
59	Survey 4	

Week 5 – What You Can Do

63	Day 1	Desire a different future
65	Day 2	Choose to lead yourself
67	Day 3	Find others to join you
69	Day 4	Be a good influence on your church family
71	Day 5	Be the best follower your leaders have ever seen
73	Survey 5	

Small Group Studies

77	1 - Being Family
80	2 - Embracing our Place
83	3 - Our Mission: To Nurture Redemptive Relationships
86	4 - Doing Mission Together as Family
89	5 - Change Begins with Me

92	A Word to Church Leaders

ABOUT THIS BOOK

This devotional is a companion to the book Redemptive Family: How church as a family, rooted in a place, lies at the heart of God's mission (Howard Webb 2020, Torn Curtain Publishing). It also forms a core part of Love Your Neighbour's Redemptive Family church series. However you came to have this booklet in your hands, our prayer is that you will be encouraged and envisioned by a biblical picture of church that is both practical and profound. You will discover a way of thinking about church that really can change the world!

— Howard Webb

WHY WE WROTE IT

What was God's purpose in establishing His church on Earth? When we are clear about the *why* of church, it becomes clearer *what* we should be doing and *how* we should be doing it.

The church is God's vehicle for making disciples who will change the world. Church that serves only itself without changing the world is like a beautiful watch that doesn't tell the time. The true measure of a church is not how many come to consume its programmes, but whether those who come are joyfully committed to serving Jesus by sharing in the mission of the church.

We can't be part of church without being part of mission. Mission is for *everyone*. We all need the thrill of discovering our purpose, of seeing our faith grow in the face of challenges, and the joy of being instrumental in leading others to Christ. For the spiritual health and growth of everyone mission must be made more human and doable and put in the hands of our people.

So here is a five-week devotional journey that will explore what it means to be a church family on a mission. Our model doesn't require special skills or lots of money and can involve everyone. The principles can be applied to any-sized church, in any place (although you will have to work out the specifics for yourselves).

ABOUT THIS BOOK

THE BIG IDEAS YOU WILL FIND IN IT

- When the church behaves as real family it proves the truth of the gospel
- Helping others experience church family for themselves is part of mission
- Jesus is our model for what mission should look and feel like
- God has already given us a place for mission
- Mission is best done together, not solo
- As mature people we need to lead ourselves

HOW TO USE IT

Ideally, your whole church family will go on this journey together and preaching will reinforce the themes of this booklet.

This booklet is designed to be used in personal devotions, but it is more than that. It is a dialogue between the people and their church leadership. At the end of every week you will find a survey cut-out page. This survey is for the benefit of your church leadership, revealing what they can do to shape your church towards this model of redemptive family.

The idea is to return the survey page to your church. The leadership will review everyone's input and give feedback to the whole church week by week.

We suggest that at the end of the Redemptive Family church series, the leadership call a forum for a church-wide conversation about the way forward.

May this journey make you alive to the ways God longs to use you and your church to glorify Him!

Howard Webb & the Love Your Neighbour team

Week 1

WE ARE A FAMILY

"THE DESCRIPTION OF THE CHURCH AS FAMILY IN THE BIBLE IS SO COMMONPLACE IT IS EASY TO OVERLOOK. FAMILY REFERENCES SUCH AS 'BROTHERS AND SISTERS' OR 'SONS AND DAUGHTERS' OR 'CHILDREN' TO ADDRESS THE CHURCH OCCUR HUNDREDS OF TIMES AND IN EVERY BOOK OF THE NEW TESTAMENT!"

WEEK 1

WHAT WE MEAN BY...

THE FAMILY TABLE

A church family needs opportunities to experience being family together. For natural families the everyday experience of family most commonly happens around the meal table. What might it look like for a church?

Some churches eat meals together. There is a lot of scriptural precedent for this. If it is also our custom to invite outsiders to this family table to enjoy a plate of food and conversation with us, our table serves both a family and a missional purpose.

If your church does not eat together some other regular, customary way of experiencing family is needed. This requires thought, intentionality and creativity. The guiding principle is that everyone who comes to you must also experience family, not just a church service.

Week 1 - Family

Day 1 - Church is called to be family

Read: Acts 2:42-47

The Bible uses a number of lovely word pictures to describe the church, but there is one stunning description of the church that is so commonplace it is easy to overlook. The church is a family! We have a Father, an older brother and around us are our brothers and sisters. Family references such 'brothers and sisters' or 'sons and daughters' or 'children' to address the church occur hundreds of times and in every book of the New Testament!

Other word pictures that describe the church as a body, or a temple, or a bride are meant metaphorically, but church as family is not purely figurative. Certainly from our reading today we can see that the earliest Christians took the call to be family quite literally. Their impulse was to sell off their possessions and to move in together to live as real family, sharing meals and working together in mission.

Being family with particular people in a particular place is meant to be 'real' and not just in some spiritual sense. This is borne out by passages that encourage us as the church to live out the values and attributes of a good, functional family:

- ★ *Put family first*
  (Galatians 6:10)

- ★ *Take pride in each other*
  (2 Corinthians 7:4)

- ★ *Have each other's back*
  (Philippians 2:4)

- ★ *Bear with each other and show forgiveness*
  (Colossians 3:13)

- ★ *The family table: a hospitable place*
  (Hebrews 13:1-2)

- ★ *Mutual accountability and encouragement*
  (Matthew 18:15-17, Hebrews 10:25)

- ★ *Practical support in hard times*
  (1 John 3:17)

- ★ *Deal with conflict*
  (Galatians 6:1-2)

Week 1 - Family

This is really important! The big idea we will be unfolding over the course of the next five weeks is that being part of a church that takes family seriously has real implications for me. It helps me find my life purpose. It helps me grow spiritually and mentor others. And mission, instead of being something that I must shoulder alone (or leave to some other church leader to do) becomes something we can all joyfully share in together.

The church at its best, relating as real family, is a beautiful thing. For the Christian it is the place where I am understood, accepted, encouraged, supported and accountable; for the not-yet-Christian it is a peek through the window at what life in the kingdom of God looks like. It is highly compelling for those with hearts hungry for God.

Reflect

1. What aspect of your church family life do you most appreciate?

_____
_____
_____
_____
_____

2. What one thing would you like to improve about your experience of church family?

_____
_____
_____
_____
_____

Prayer:
Dear Lord, thank you for my adoption into the family of God and for the church family I am a part of. Please open my eyes and my heart to see and experience my church as family. Where I have grown accustomed to facing life alone, teach me my need of the brothers and sisters you have given me. Grow my concern for their welfare, both physically and spiritually and help me to discern when I might give them words of challenge, comfort or Encouragement. Amen.

Week 1 - Family

Day 2 - A family knows me and Needs me to contribute

Read: Galatians 6:1-10

Who knows our story better than our own family? We can sometimes pretend to be someone we are not to those that know us less well, but family has a way of quickly bringing us back down to earth!

From today's passage we learn that when church is true family, we know the good and the bad of each other's story well enough for sinful attitudes to be confronted in love and for restoration and forgiveness to be freely sought and given. Here too is where helpful words of wisdom can instruct us and where our sincere efforts and good works can be mutually encouraged. All of this knocks the rough edges off us and helps us grow spiritually. Such deep knowing of each other only comes from spending time together and being willing out of love for the other to press into uncomfortable territory despite the possibility of causing offence.

In a regular family everyone makes a contribution. The role of each family member shapes the dynamic of the family so that without them the family will be different.

Paul uses the metaphor of the body to describe how this is true for the church family also. Some of us are eyes, feet, noses – each with a unique purpose (1 Cor. 12:12-31). He points out that we, the various body parts, form one body in which we all belong to each other; and we are each given different gifts according to God's grace which we are to exercise for the benefit of the whole family (Romans 12:5-8). Only the church family provides the space for us to both usefully minister to others and be ministered to in this way.

God intends both for the family to grow spiritually and to fulfil His purposes in the world. In an individualistic culture we can sometimes read verses that were written to whole churches and take only a personal application from them. Read the following passage with your 'family' glasses on, understanding that the words 'you' and 'your' are all plural:

Week 1 - Family

Philippians 2:12-16 says "Work hard to show the results of your salvation, obeying God with deep reverence and fear. For God is working in you, giving you the desire and the power to do what pleases him. Do everything without complaining and arguing, so that no one can criticize you. Live clean, innocent lives as children of God, shining like bright lights in a world full of crooked and perverse people. Hold firmly to the word of life; then, on the day of Christ's return, I will be proud that I did not run the race in vain and that my work was not useless."

Paul wants the church to be on this journey together as family. In doing so they will fulfil God's purposes in the world and be a light to their world. God gave you a family. Determine today that you want to mine the richness of this wonderful gift.

Reflect

1. Who from my church family knows me well enough to know my weaknesses?

_____
_____
_____
_____
_____
_____

2 Is there someone being excluded in my church whom I could help belong?

_____
_____
_____
_____
_____

Prayer:
Dear Lord, thank you for the gift of a family that can minister to me when I am needy and which helps me also minister to others. Forgive me for sometimes being too rushed or self-focused to spend the time I should with others in the family. Help me to see them with the eyes of Jesus as worthy and beautiful. Please grow our sense of oneness. Reveal Your purposes for this family in the place where you have planted us. Amen.

Week 1 - Family

Day 3 - Healthy Church Family is a Powerful Witness

Read: Matthew 5:14-16

This is another passage we must read with our 'family' glasses on. Once again 'you' and 'your' are plural words.

In this passage Jesus looks at the future leaders of his church and tells them that the things they will do together will be seen by others as evidence of God at work. The 'city on a hill' imagery of a myriad twinkling lights gathered in one place shining out into the darkness is a beautiful picture of how we together as family are the light of the world.

Jesus also said that the watching world would know that we are His disciples because they observe two marvelous characteristics: they will marvel at our love for each other (John 13:35) and they will marvel at our unity (John 17:23). He anticipated that onlookers would see the gathered church being real family and be drawn to it.

There is no finer example of the saving power of a real church family than the passage with which we began the week, Acts 2:42-47. It is worth revisiting again:

> "All the believers devoted themselves to the apostles' teaching, and to fellowship, and to sharing in meals (including the Lord's Supper), and to prayer. A deep sense of awe came over them all, and the apostles performed many miraculous signs and wonders. And all the believers met together in one place and shared everything they had. They sold their property and possessions and shared the money with those in need. They worshiped together at the Temple each day, met in homes for the Lord's Supper, and shared their meals with great joy and generosity—all the while praising God and enjoying the goodwill of all the people. And each day the Lord added to their fellowship those who were being saved."

Week 1 - Family

Notice the cycle between the public spaces (temple and marketplace) where ordinary people gathered; and their homes, where they gathered as church family. Through invitation and hospitality outsiders met a family on fire for God. People were saved and the family grew.

Our church family may be a powerful witness, but how will outsiders know unless they get a chance to experience us? The answer still lies in invitation and hospitality. The family that wants to grow needs empty seats at the family table that they are longing to fill. As guests experience a loving family and return again and again they may become family too.

Reflect

1. **Have I ever experienced unconditional acceptance? What did it feel like?**

_____
_____
_____
_____
_____

2 **What opportunities for invitation and hospitality does my church family provide?**

_____
_____
_____
_____
_____

Prayer:

Dear Lord, today I raise up to You my church family. I pray that when outsiders get an inside view of us worshipping and serving you, that they will be struck by the sweetness of our love and unity and will be conscious of the fact that 'God is here'. Make me conscious of the role I play in the culture of our church family. Help me to look beyond my circle of close friends to the newcomer and to welcome them in a way that will make You smile. And quicken my mind to opportunities that arise to invite those in my personal world to experience my church family also. Amen.

Week 1 – Family

Day 4 – Mission is meant to be done together as family

Read: Ephesians 4:1-16

Today's passage beautifully illustrates how, as we work on being Christ's family together in the power and strength of the Spirit, we together are equipped for works of service which in turn helps us all grow and mature. When we together are doing the good works for which we were created and which God planned long ago for us to do (Eph 2:10) we are doing mission.

In the West we tend to imagine ourselves as lone rangers on a personal mission in our individual worlds, with church as a kind of refuelling station. Mission described in the New Testament is usually undertaken by a group of individuals; the exceptions are always due to special circumstances (such as Paul being in prison, or Philip being carried into the desert). Our encounters with the people whom God sends across our path begin with just us, but we need to know that this relationship is one our church family also cares about and wants to share.

Mission is the process by which those we befriend in our world become part of the family of God. God is already at work in the life of the people we meet; our part of the process starts with personal befriending and then, through hospitality and invitation (and the application of godly wisdom) we introduce them to our Christian family friends, trusting that by God's grace we will woo them to our church family table.

This approach to mission isn't only more doable, it is sensible. Relationships can be hard work. All of us have only limited capacity to add new relationships to our lives, especially if they are 'high need'. However, if we can share our relationships with others in our church family then we can befriend many more people between us. This has the double benefit of immediately introducing our seeking friend to a wider network of Christians, thereby multiplying the number of 'God conversations' they will have and making it far more likely that they will take the leap of faith.

Week 1 - Family

There's also a bigger question. When I lead someone to Christ, what's next? Ahead lies a lifelong process of discipleship. I cannot do this alone. I need my church family to be welcoming and willing to change shape in order to include my new disciple so that they can enjoy the life-changing reality of being part of the family themselves.

The aim of the gospel is to bring people into relationship with Jesus and His church. Experiencing the reality of a community who passionately loves God, each other and the not-yet-saved can win over the hearts of the lost before their heads have even fully comprehended the message of salvation. As they journey with us their understanding will grow; and the truth is, the good news continues to get bigger and bigger for every Christian as we grow in the grace and knowledge of Jesus.

Let's remember that it was God's plan to put us in church families where everyone can play their part and exercise the special, miraculous gifts that God has given them — not only for the benefit of those already within the faith, but also for the redemption of those on the outside looking in.

Reflect

1. **Who has God brought across my path that I could grow a relationship with?**

   _____
   _____
   _____

2. **Who from my church family would I be happy to introduce this person to?**

   _____
   _____
   _____

Prayer:

Dear Lord, thank you that I don't need to feel like a 'lone ranger' in mission, having to do everything myself. I am grateful for the giftings, wisdom and different life experiences of everyone else in my church family which can complement what I can do or say in pointing others to Jesus. Help me and the rest of my church family to embrace this way of thinking and please open our eyes to all the ways we can mutually support each other's relationships with outsiders. Amen.

WEEK 1 - FAMILY

DAY 5 - THE PEOPLE IN OUR WORLD NEED A FAMILY

Read: Luke 5:17-26

In today's reading, we encounter an invalid who is very lucky to have a cohort of friends who care for him like family. Finding it impossible to get in they could have given up, knowing that at least they tried. But this man's friends loved him more. They were prepared to do something unexpected (and potentially expensive) to get him the help he needed. We all need friends like that.

We have an epidemic of loneliness in New Zealand society. We all crave deep connection with other human beings with whom we can share our story but we live in a self-focused, attention-deficit world. Surveys reveal that the number of close friends the average person relates to has probably halved in the last 20 years.

It turns out the "friends" orbiting at the farthest reaches of our digital galaxy can't solve our real-world loneliness. The vital friendships — the people we hug and laugh and cry with and who know the unvarnished truth about us — are the ones who have the greatest impact on our health and happiness.

Peter Drucker was a famous consultant, educator and author, credited with establishing modern business management practice. He observed that everyone needs the three C's : Community, Commitment and Contribution. We all need deep connection to others, we need commitment to a cause that is greater than ourselves and we all need to know that our contribution makes a difference.

The lonely people in our world need a family where they can belong, have a purpose and contribute their unique gifting. Who other than the church family is willing to offer this kind of radical, messy, time-consuming hospitality? Taking the time to hear the story of our neighbours and relating their story to the story of Jesus is perhaps the greatest missional opportunity of our age.

Week 1 - Family

Churches often fret about being seen as relevant by the local community. But it is not meeting the cultural expectations of those around us that makes us relevant. It is our unconditional love for those we invite to the family table and our constancy in living out the values of the kingdom together that make us 'a city on a hill.'

As we draw the first week of this devotional series to a close, let us take a last look at the picture of a church family we painted together.

- The church family should be a place where I can be known and loved and can make a contribution
- The church family should welcome outsiders to come and witness the reality of church family life together
- The church family should be mutually encouraging and supportive of the relationships we each have with not-yet-Christians.

Reflect

1. How does my church meet my need for community, contribution and commitment?

_____
_____
_____
_____

2. What could we do together to address the loneliness around us?

_____
_____
_____
_____

Prayer:

Dear Lord, save me from the pitfalls of a society that values freedom, individuality and independence above all else and ends up being lonely. Help us as your church to seek the healthy interdependence of family that you intended for us, in which we can share each other's burdens. Thank you for the church family you have given me. When next I feel detained or irritated by someone in the family, remind me Lord that they are a precious gift from you and I should take the time to appreciate the gift. Amen.

Week 1 - Family

Survey 1

This survey will help inform your church leadership as they consider how best to support the vision of church as redemptive family. Cut out this page and return it to church. Your church leadership will provide ongoing feedback through the course of the series.

1. What aspect of our church family life do you most appreciate?

_____
_____
_____
_____
_____
_____
_____

2. What can we do in our Sunday service to improve our experience of family?

_____
_____
_____
_____
_____
_____
_____

3. How can we change how we communicate to improve our experience of family?

_____
_____
_____
_____
_____

Week 1 - Family

4. How can we improve our experience of family by the things we do together?

5. What else have you been prompted about this week?

Week 2

WE ARE A FAMILY IN A PLACE

"WHEN WE ARE BLIND TO THE VERY PLACE GOD PLANTED US WE SEVERELY HAMPER OUR ABILITY TO PARTNER WITH GOD ON MISSION, BECAUSE MISSION IS ALWAYS TO PARTICULAR PEOPLE IN A PARTICULAR PLACE. WHY SHOULD OUR MISSION NOT BE TO THE PEOPLE IN THE PLACE WHERE WE ARE ALREADY?"

Week 2

WHAT WE MEAN BY...

Shalom

Most know that the Hebrew word *shalom* means 'peace.' Our English word describes an absence of strife or war, but this ancient word has a greater richness of meaning.

According to Strong's Concordance *shalom* means completeness, wholeness, health, peace, welfare, safety, soundness, tranquility, prosperity, perfection, fullness, rest, harmony and the absence of agitation or discord.

When we seek God's *shalom* for our community we are seeking more than peace; we are seeking a completeness and restoration that can only fully be found under the reign and lordship of Jesus.

Week 2 - Place

Day 1 - God has a purpose for our church Family being where it is

Read: Acts 17:24-28

It is no accident that your church family finds itself planted in a particular local community. It's an unusual passage, but I read today's devotional scripture as saying that God marked out the times *and the places* we would live so that we would be there for those wanting to reach out and find God. Ask yourself this: if your church family isn't going to be a conduit of God's blessing to its neighbours, then who is?

We learn from Scripture that God not only cares for us as individuals, but also cares about our places of belonging – our communities, towns and cities. Three poignant passages that spring to mind are Jonah 4:11 where God tells how deeply he cares for Nineveh, Jeremiah 29:7 in which God's people are instructed to seek the peace and prosperity of their city, and Luke 19:41-44 where Jesus is moved to tears by the predicament of Jerusalem.

One of the first questions we ask of someone new is, "Where are you from?" We ask the question because knowing where they belong tells us something important about them. A stranger is someone without a place, someone who has come from a place where they did belong and are now rootless in a place where they don't yet belong. If we are really meant to be a family on a mission, where is this family when it is home? Where does our church family belong?

Chances are your church family was planted in a place where there was a felt need for a church. The founders no doubt thought, "This place needs a church like ours". But over time some churches lose this vision of being a blessing to their place. Congregants drive to buildings to enjoy great teaching or great worship and then drive home, forgetting the call to be good neighbours. Metaphorically they let weeds grow in the place where God planted them because they no longer own it as their place. They are no longer receiving the place where they are planted as a gift from the hand of God Himself.

Week 2 - Place

Every church family exists within a culture and we tend to bring the values of our culture into church with us. One of those values is a constant striving for better or for more. Discontent is very human. Because of the ease with which we can now travel great distances we fall prey to escapist thinking that something better or more suitable may be found in some other place. Instead of dreaming about the ordinary places we know, we dream and hope for the extraordinary somewhere else.

We can only know ourselves rightly when we first know our God. And we only know Him rightly when we know Him as sovereign Lord of all creation, who gives us our place as a gift. When we are blind to the very place God planted us we severely hamper our ability to partner with God on mission, because mission is always to particular people in a particular place. Unless God has called us as missionaries to people in another place, why should our mission not be to the people in the place where we are already?

Reflect

1. What do you know of your church family's roots? Why is your church where it is?

_____
_____
_____
_____

2 Is your church family responsive to the place where it is? What might help?

_____
_____
_____
_____

Prayer:

Dear Lord, today I reflect on the fact that the place where I am now is becoming part of my own life story and is helping shape my identity. Forgive me for the times I am discontent and fail to see the extraordinary King waiting to bring this ordinary place under His rule. May I not only be shaped by this place, but in turn leave my imprint on it as a child of God. Help me to become one of the voices reminding my church family that this too is a place where the Son of God walks and that He has planted our church family here to bring Him glory in this place. Amen.

WEEK 2 - PLACE

Day 2 - Embracing our Place

Read: Jeremiah 29:4-14

The overarching story of the Old Testament is of how God rescued His homeless people Israel and gave them land and a home. When God later instructs them to care for strangers and aliens it is a reminder that Israel were once exactly that themselves. God doesn't want us to live rootless lives. As today's reading also emphasises, rootedness in place and community is God's design.

The church is not a collection of individuals who choose to associate to have their spiritual needs met, but a community participating both in the life of Jesus and the life of the world. To fulfil our purpose as a church family we need to embrace the place in the world where God has planted us.

The Father is a gardener, and every place is like a garden. A garden has to have boundaries. Careful planting, watering and tending within the confines of the garden can turn a barren wasteland into a beautiful, fruitful place that nurtures the soul and is a delight for those who enjoy it. Kingdom transformation can begin in a place where a church family is faithfully present over time.

The boundaries of a particular place help us by limiting our scope and focusing our efforts. We can't be everywhere and do everything; putting a frame around our mission sets us free to invest deeply in one place. Of course, place is more than location; what makes place is the complex interaction of lives with each other and with the land in a particular location.

Churches who are blind to place must keep asking the questions 'what should we do?' and 'where should we do it?' By contrast, when our church family (whatever its size) is rooted in the place where God has planted us, our mission field lies readily to hand. What should we do? We simply ask what evangelism, creation care and forging *shalom* look like in this community that we are coming to know. Where should we do it? Right here of course!

Week 2 - Place

This understanding lies at the heart of the rich concept of 'parish'. At the heart of parish is a church family living out its faith together, creating a web of relationships in the community. From the perspective of those outside church, the parish creates an open space where I can belong and be welcome simply by virtue of sharing place with the church family. As the church family lives out the gospel so that others may belong not only to the parish but to the family too, some will be moved from belonging to believing.

As we experience a place from the inside out we begin to invest in it. A church family exerts influence on a neighbourhood when it sees the value in this role. But embracing our place requires that we be 'dug in' and turn towards our community with openness and hope.

Reflect

1. **What do you love about the place where God has planted you?**

_____
_____
_____
_____
_____

2. **Who do you know who speaks out on behalf of your community? What could they tell your church family about the place where they are planted?**

_____
_____
_____
_____
_____

Prayer:

Dear Lord, thank you that you haven't made it our individual responsibility to change the whole world, only to take spiritual responsibility for the place where we are. Thank you for the freedom and clarity that having boundaries gives us! Sometimes it seems we look everywhere else except immediately around us. Help me to see the place that gives me part of my own identity with new eyes of hope and faith that Your Kingdom can break through here. Amen.

Week 2 - Place

Day 3 - Growing local relationships

Read: Luke 4:38 - 5:11

You may have thought as I did that Jesus stepping into Peter's boat to preach in Luke 5 was a random 'God moment', but looking back at Luke 4 we see that it was not. Jesus first meets Peter in the synagogue, then at Peter's home where He heals his mother-in-law. Now when He encounters Peter by the shore it is perfectly natural that Jesus would ask a friend to use his boat.

Relationships flourish through regular encounters. Multiple touches are essential if relationships are to deepen. Relationships grow even quicker when someone is befriended by several people who already have strong relational ties to each other. Being cared for by a group of friends is affirming and encouraging and introduces one to a whole network of relationships.

When we commit to be a blessing to our place, it makes sense that we live as much of our everyday life as possible in our community. This means that more of us will be shopping locally, frequenting the local coffee shops, joining the local sports and community clubs and taking an active interest in local affairs. Not only will we be enriching our relationships with those who live in our parish, but we will be seeing more of each other too and our family bonds will deepen.

What does this commitment to a place look like? It is being willing to stand in line longer at the supermarket in order to say a few words to the checkout operator you have had past conversations with. Commitment may be costlier - it may mean choosing to move house so you can live in the parish your church family is serving.

Thinking 'parish' helps our church family model successful mission. Real mission is journeying with people to faith. This implies that we get to know them and grow with them over time. The experience of walking alongside those coming to faith gives us skills and grows our faith, which we can then pass on to others (Phil. 4:9). This is true discipleship.

Week 2 - Place

There is natural continuity of relationship in a parish, because it is where the church family and the people who live in that place both choose to be present. Without a focus on parish what passes for mission is often a feel-good event with strangers we won't meet again, trusting that the small seed we sowed will somehow be watered by someone else and grow. Do we really want to settle for this as a picture of what successful mission looks like?

Reaching neighbourhoods is the only way to reach everyone. When we only reach out to affinity groups — the young, the old, those with young children, business people, the homeless — we miss seeing their web of natural connections to others. Consequently, we will never touch most of the people in our orbit. Missionary theologian Leslie Newbigin says, "The geographical parish can never become irrelevant or marginal. The primary sense of neighbourhood must remain primary, because it is here that men and women relate to each other simply as human beings and not in respect of their functions in society." In other words, it is in the neighbourhoods of our parish that we have the possibility of engaging richly with everyone.

Reflect

1. What did I find challenging in today's devotional? What questions do I have?

_____
_____
_____

2 Who in my community can I deepen a relationship with today?

_____
_____
_____

Prayer:

Dear Lord, I would like to be part of the journey to faith of several people in my community. Forgive me for the times I have been blind to the opportunities before me. As I encounter people regularly in my place please open my eyes to see them as you do and to begin building relational bridges with them. Bring to mind also those from my church family who could be sharing the relational journey with me. Amen.

Week 2 – Place

Day 4 – Restoring our place

Read: 2 Corinthians 5:11-21, Romans 8:18-30

Today's passage from 2 Corinthians speaks of our God-given role as relationship-restorers in our world, and the verses from Romans add something profound. The good news of the Kingdom is not just for people; all of creation is in bondage because of the curse of sin. This physical world, of which our place is a part, also waits and longs to be restored when God's Kingdom is revealed.

We do not pray to be delivered *out* of this world, but rather that God will bring healing and salvation *to* our world. Rather than seeking to save disembodied souls *out* of creation, we cooperate with God in redeeming *all* of creation. The good news at the heart of our mission is big enough to speak to all aspects of human flourishing; our personal salvation, as well as social justice and creation care. As we seek to bring the people and the land of our place back into right relationship with each other and with God, God's *shalom* can reign there.

We need to cultivate a holy imagination. With the eye of faith we need to see beyond the present reality to what our place could be and one day will be under the lordship of Jesus. How can we pray 'your Kingdom come, your will be done on earth' if we have no idea what we are asking for? The change must begin with God's people living out this future vision. We proclaim the gospel, and also choose to live counter-culturally in ways that are ecologically responsible and do not hurt or exploit others.

We need to be place-makers. A homemaker makes a house a home by transforming space with their distinctive personal touch. A home is a place of peace. It draws you in and makes you want to linger. Just so the Spirit of Jesus moves us to be place-makers until the place where God has planted us reflects His *shalom*. Our work in place-making and culture-creating reflects the renewed and healed Jerusalem when Jesus returns to make everything right (Rev. 22).

We are called to be instruments of God's peace. The consequences of sin have disrupted the relationships in our place. Our neighbours are out of relationship with God; and there is self-centredness and self-interest at the heart of every local dispute and in every systemic injustice.

Week 2 - Place

Once our own hearts are right with God, God gives us the message of reconciliation to share with others (2 Corinthians 5). This message of reconciliation tears down walls so that those who once lived as enemies can live together in peace.

A vital part of our ministry of reconciliation is the clear proclamation of the message of salvation found in Jesus. Jesus said, what good is it if one gains the whole world but loses one's soul? (Mark 8:36). We call to our place, "Be reconciled to God!" The only change that will last is centred in Him.

We also strive to reconcile people with each other. Where there is poverty, injustice, oppression or lack of mercy, a wall has been erected that separates people from right relationship. Jesus cares so deeply about these issues that He includes them in His own ministry manifesto, so we should too (see Luke 4:16-20).

When we serve as instruments of God's love we bear witness to the King who reigns over our place.

Reflect

1. **What aspect of the good news (salvation, justice or creation care) have we as a church overlooked in our place/parish?**

_____
_____
_____

2. **What could we do with the people in our place so that they not only experience something of the Kingdom but are pointed to the King?**

_____
_____
_____

Prayer:

Dear Lord, today we have been thinking about how You wish to bring healing not only to me, my natural family or even my church family, but to the whole place where I live. Help me and my church family to do what You require – to humble ourselves, to seek after You and to be ambassadors for the whole gospel in our place. I pray that the witness of a church earnestly on its knees for the redemption of the place where You have planted us will be used by Your Spirit to stir hearts and turn them to You. Amen.

Week 2 - Place

Day 5 - Persevering for the Sake of our place

Read: Revelation 3:7-13

Over two weeks we have built up a picture of a church family living out its faith together in the place God has planted them. The vision of how we might embrace our place and see it transformed is inspiring. But if we imagine that this will be an easy, feel-good exercise resulting in everyone loving us, we may be in for a rude awakening. Reality is seldom like that. In fact, Scripture warns us that when we live an authentic, counter-cultural life we can expect to be misunderstood, have our motivations questioned and our character maligned (2 Tim. 3:12). As a church family we have to decide: are we seeking to be popular, or are we seeking to reflect the Kingdom without compromise?

In today's passage the church in Philadelphia is commended for remaining true to their calling and for not giving up, despite facing headwinds and having little strength.

Rather than seeking to be liked we need to exhort each other to be courageous and resilient. Resilience is the ability to bounce back from challenging events or overcome obstacles that get in the way of us achieving our goals and to keep enduring. Our resilience is rooted in the security of our relationship with God through Jesus, not in the circumstances around us. We are here to love our world, whether our community likes us or not.

Picture a mother feeding her baby solids for the first time. She scoops up food in the spoon and pops it into the baby's mouth. The baby, who is unused to these flavours and textures spits most of it out again. What does the mother do? She is not fazed by the baby's apparent lack of gratitude. She continues to persevere until the baby is full. Why? Because she is committed to doing the best for the child entrusted to her care.

Enduring resilience in respect of ministry in and to our place is important both for us and for our neighbours. If I am not sure I will be here tomorrow, why should I invest my life? If my neighbour is unsure that I will be here tomorrow, why should he tell me who he is and what he cares about?

Week 2 – Place

Real relationships come about through multiple encounters over time. Relationships can also be bumpy and fraught. But unless we endure and spend the time we will never take our relationships to a deeper level where engaging in redemptive God-conversations becomes possible.

Living as church family embracing a parish with no endpoint is challenging. As the saying goes, we can't fool all the people all the time. Is our faith more than just talk? As we live transparently with our neighbours they will discern for themselves whether our love for each other and for them is able to stand the test of time.

Reflect

1. How much of my Christian service to others is driven by a need to be liked?

_____
_____
_____
_____
_____
_____

2. How does 'being in the same boat' with our church family help me to be courageous and resilient?

_____
_____
_____
_____
_____

Prayer:

Dear Lord, help me to care more about hearing 'Well done, good and faithful servant' from You than hearing nice things said about me by others. Grant me the courage to demonstrate true love for those around me by addressing the real issues and talking about what really matters. Help me to accept the dare to my faith of living my Christian walk transparently before others so that they might see your grace filling up my weakness. May those that look in on my life discover their deep thirst to also enjoy that eternal spring of living water within them that You give Your children. Amen.

WEEK 2 – PLACE

SURVEY 2

This survey will help inform your church leadership as they consider how best to support the vision of church as redemptive family. Cut out this page and return it to church. Your church leadership will provide ongoing feedback through the course of the series.

1. Can you tell us a story about our church being a 'city on a hill' in our community?

_____
_____
_____
_____
_____
_____
_____

2. What can we do / What can we change to establish a faithful presence in our 'parish'?
(You don't have to provide an answer in every category)

a. What we do in our Sunday service

_____
_____
_____
_____
_____
_____

b. How we communicate

_____
_____
_____
_____
_____
_____

Week 2 – Place

c. The things we do together

d. How we use our buildings and facilities

e. Something else

Week 3

WE ARE A FAMILY IN A PLACE ON A MISSION

"WHAT IS THE MECHANISM BY WHICH PEOPLE FROM THE COMMUNITY ARE GOING TO COME IN TO EXPERIENCE CHURCH FAMILY FROM THE INSIDE OUT? THE ANSWER IS YOU. YOU ARE THE PATHWAY BY WHICH OTHERS WILL BE LED TO EXPERIENCE THE CHURCH FAMILY."

Week 3

WHAT WE MEAN BY...

Nurturing Redemptive Relationships

'Nurturing' speaks to our mindfulness in relationships, and to our motivation of love and care.

'Redemptive' describes the God-glorifying quality of our relationships and how they lead others closer to Jesus.

'Relationships' lie at the heart of mission. The church is called to make disciples, relationally engaged with God, their church family and the world.

Week 3 - Mission

Day 1 - Your relationships are Your church's mission

Read: 1 Thessalonians 3:12 - 4:12

So far we have seen that a true church family that embraces the geographical place in which it is planted is poised to be a powerful witness and to fulfil God's purposes. But how will it happen? What is the mechanism by which people from the community are going to come in to experience church family from the inside out?

The answer is you. You are the pathway by which others will be led in to experience the church family. Your role is not merely to support your church organisation in its mission – the bigger part is having your church family supporting you in mission! 1 Thess. 3:12 says, 'May the Lord make your love for one another and for all people grow and overflow, just as our love for you overflows.' It is by loving each other enough to also love the 'all people' we each bring to the family table that we form a redemptive pathway that leads from parish to church and back out again.

This is how it works. As a Spirit-filled believer, you befriend those you encounter in your world, seeking through example and conversation to woo them closer to Jesus. Through hospitality and invitation you grow their relational network of other Christians by introducing them to others in your church family. Together you then draw them to the church family table, where their coming has been anticipated and will be celebrated. There they experience authentic Christian family, hear the gospel preached and also hear the first-hand stories of the power of God in changing lives. Convicted by the Holy Spirit they repent and become Christ-followers too, thereby growing the family which in turn grows them and supports them in mission.

The scenario described above is not likely to happen in this picture-perfect way. Real life and imperfect people will cause detours from the ideal path. However, this simple missional blueprint is reflected in the book of Acts and throughout the New Testament and works in every context, even in places where the church faces persecution.

Week 3 - Mission

In this model every church family member has a purpose and role to play. Real-world mentoring and discipleship (and accountability too) is built in as we participate together and learn from each other. As our expectancy that God will move in the hearts and lives of the unsaved is proved correct, our faith grows.

Doesn't contemplating this model stir and excite you? It is true that some changes may have to be made to exactly how we do church. The beauty of working through this material as a church family is that, if we agree, making the changes needed should not be difficult. The shape of every church family is after all determined by the family itself!

Let your daily reflections prompt you to dream about what could and should be. Since God wants your church to be fruitful and growing, trust that He will bring about His purposes.

Reflect

1. **Does this model of doing mission alarm or excite me?**

_____
_____
_____
_____

2 **What could your church do to encourage doing mission this way?**

_____
_____
_____
_____

Prayer:

Dear Lord, I have reflected today on how I and my church family could be a team in helping people find Jesus. I pray for everyone from my church family who will be challenged by our reading today; may we take what is hopeful and true from this idea of how mission works and find new ways of partnering together in mission. Help us to be bold and courageous in doing our own part; but thank You that You have given us a whole church family to help share the load. Amen.

WEEK 3 - MISSION

DAY 2 - YOUR MISSION IS A PERFECT FIT FOR YOU

Read: 1 John 4: 7-21

Today's passage reminds us that God is love and that love for God and others lies at the heart of mission. Elsewhere, Jesus summed up what it means to be a Christ-follower with these two commands: to love the Lord our God with all our heart, all your soul, and all your mind and to love our neighbour as ourselves (Matthew 22:36-40).

God demonstrated what our mission is to be like by sending His son Jesus to model it for us. Mission for Jesus looked like 24/7 discipleship. It looked like eating with sinners. It was Jesus saying 'Today I have called you friends'. It was Jesus choosing to lay down His life for those who were still in rebellion against God.

Some experience 'mission' as a cold, prickly word because of their past experiences. Bad experiences happen when we try and force mission into a box of our own creation. When we force mission into a time box or into a method box, 'doing mission' can become our focus, rather than expressing and demonstrating God's love to the person before us.

'Mission' should describe the ways we relate to outsiders that is just like Jesus. It should be kind, respectful and relational - an expression of our best selves and not something we are later ashamed of. Mission is something we can all participate in as Jesus' body on earth and still be our authentic selves.

In the model of missional church we are exploring together through this devotional series we can define personal mission as nurturing redemptive relationships in our world; and the mission of our church family is to help support the redemptive relationships of each of its family members. Mission is not an occasional duty or obligation but the core purpose of my church family. It should be natural and relational and part of my everyday experience, rather than awkward and uncomfortable.

Week 3 - Mission

What do we mean by a redemptive relationship? It is a relationship of friendship in which I commit to seek God's best for the other person. I am prayerfully alive to opportunities presented by the Spirit of God over time to woo my friend closer to Jesus through words, deeds and answers to prayer. I want my friend to experience my church family and come to faith so that they too can grow in God and enjoy Him forever.

This looks less like shouting on a street corner or tracts on a windscreen and more like meals and conversations at your house. It is less about controlling conversations and more about relationships. Caring for someone else opens up the possibility that you will be hurt. This is part of what it means to be fully human in mission. But we can draw comfort and encouragement from the fact that we are on this exciting adventure together as family.

Reflect

1. *How do I feel about a life not focused on me?*

_____
_____
_____
_____
_____

2. *What wrong thinking do I have to overcome about happiness and the purpose of life?*

_____
_____
_____
_____
_____

Prayer:

Dear Lord, it is so tempting to seek worldly success and pleasures on the one hand, and to still want to hear Your commendation on the other. Please heal my divided heart. I acknowledge Lord that You created me and that all I am and have is really Yours. Help me every day to choose to live for You rather than for myself. Help me to find my joy and satisfaction in being a truly human redemptive influence in my world and in my church family. Amen.

Week 3 - Mission

Day 3 - Beginning a Redemptive relationship

Read: Philippians 4:4-9

Today's passage describes the kind of person you and I would love to meet – someone who is kind, gentle and wholesome and sees the best in the other person. God asks us to be that someone.

Before a relationship can be redemptive (by wooing someone to Jesus), a relationship has to exist. We need to move through our day in prayerful openness to the possibility that God has destined an encounter for us this day. It may be someone with whom we already have a superficial relationship, or someone we are meeting for the first time. Signal your willingness to be their friend and see what happens next!

Doug Pollock in his book *God Space* (available from Love Your Neighbour) gives practical advice on the very human ways we can sensitively and graciously begin relationship-building.

Noticing

Every person we meet is someone loved by God and made in His image. An important first step is just being interested enough to take the time to really notice them. There is something interesting about everyone. How is it that you are presently sharing the same space? Are they happy or sad? Are they wearing a brooch, a watch or a tattoo that intrigues you? There is a story associated with all of these things – invite them to tell it to you. Prove your interest by remembering and referencing what they tell you next time! You may want to jot down notes after a meeting to help your memory.

Listening

We can have so much to say that we miss the clues the other person is giving us about where they are at. Listening communicates humility and respect. Really listening often gives us the pick-up points to have the conversations that matter about life and God.

Week 3 - Mission

Doug Pollock says: "Nothing creates God Space faster than Spirit-led listening. When we demonstrate that we are truly seeking to understand people – not simply change their point of view – we create a safe environment that allows them to open up at a deeper level. As others feel genuinely understood, they also begin to better understand themselves" (pg. 56).

Serving

Buying them a coffee or staying after hours to help them get a job done are some ways that we indicate that we care enough about them to follow up words with actions. Giving up your spare time to help them communicates that they matter. It also enriches our relationship by increasing our pool of common experience. But our primary motive in serving is not to manipulate – it is choosing to do what Jesus would do.

Reflect

1. **Who is God prompting me to notice?**

_____
_____
_____
_____
_____
_____

2. **How could I start using the tools of noticing, listening and serving?**

_____
_____
_____
_____
_____
_____

Prayer:

Dear Lord, help me today to be someone who is kind, gentle, wholesome and positive. Open my eyes to see the opportunities for connection that I may have been missing. I pray that today I will get the opportunity to practise noticing, listening or serving. Amen.

Week 3 - Mission

Day 4 - Spiritual conversations

Read: Romans 1:8-17

Paul says in today's passage 'I am not ashamed of this Good News about Christ. It is the power of God at work, saving everyone who believes' (v.16).

God created all human beings in His image and we all wonder about God. It would be strange to deny this human side of us and to choose never to talk about spiritual things. As Christ-followers living out the reality of our spiritual rebirth, why would we hide this vitally important aspect of our lives from our friend when they are thinking about God too?

The practices of noticing, listening and serving that we looked at yesterday all lead to conversations, which in turn open our eyes to what God is already doing in the life of the person with whom we are engaging. If we are prayerfully seeking an opportunity, the time and space for a God conversation will naturally (or perhaps supernaturally!) arise – on God's timetable, rather than ours.

What does a spiritual conversation look like?

It will be curious and respectful of what your friend believes and feels. In *God Space* Doug Pollock talks about asking 'wondering' questions. When you have been told something that piques your curiosity, or you have provoked a strong reaction by something you have said, you could ask: 'I am wondering about what you said/how you reacted. Is there a story around that?' This is a way of going deeper and may be a way to get back into a conversation even much later!

It will be a truthful witness of your own experience without being long and preachy. Avoid the temptation of over-selling what it means to be a Christian. Coming to Christ didn't make us perfect or our lives completely problem-free. Honesty and sincerity are the surest way to draw our friend in closer, rather than push them away. Also resist the pressure to tell them the whole story of your life – it is much better to prepare little story capsules of key moments in your Christian journey and use them as appropriate.

Week 3 - Mission

It will leave your friend clearer on what it means to be a Christ-follower. At some stage you will want your friend to hear and understand the way of salvation. Whether *you* share it, they hear it from someone else in your church family, or they hear it on your church's Alpha course is not the most important question. What is important is that they experience a true Christ-follower firsthand – that's you! One powerful witness is offering to pray for the situation they find themselves in, just as you would for yourself. It includes God in your relationship and makes a follow-up conversation about what happened perfectly natural.

Next week we will be reflecting on how we might share our relationships with others in our church family. You need not feel that you must carry the burden of mission all alone; doing mission together is the biblical pattern. Relax into it and enjoy the journey!

Reflect

1. Have I ever been tempted to make the Christian walk seem like a bed of roses? Why is this?

_____
_____
_____
_____
_____

2 If I was to share a recent reality of my Christian experience with a new friend, what would it be?

_____
_____
_____
_____

Prayer:

Dear Lord, help me to care about the people in my world enough that I will forget about myself and my own particular hang-ups in order to take a genuine interest in their story. Help me to see how You are already at work in the lives and circumstances of the people I get to talk to today. Where there is opportunity to share a bit of my God story, give me the courage and sensitivity to do it well. Amen.

Week 3 – Mission

Day 5 – What about those I cannot connect to my church family?

Read: 1 Corinthians 3:6-9

Today's passage makes the point that some get to plant the Word while others get to water, but it is God who makes it grow.

Let's say we progress to having spiritual conversations with someone we can't connect to our own church family for whatever reason. How should we think about this relationship? In such a situation it is important that we listen to what the Spirit is saying to us, because every relationship is unique. We should not however be guided by wrong thinking.

We alone can't be church for them. We alone don't have the words, the wisdom, the life experiences, the Scripture knowledge or the giftings that a whole church body can share. Ongoing discipleship happens best when we share life together as a church family.

We may be bearing the burden of thinking that we are this person's only spiritual lifeline and that their whole eternal destiny rests on us. We may even be attracted to this picture because of the importance it places on our personal role. We need to change this narrative, because God is at the centre of the story. It is the work of the Holy Spirit in our friend's life that we are having spiritual conversations today. We are only a link in the chain, joining what God has done in this person's life in the past with what He will do in the future.

What then does God expect of us? Firstly, He expects us to fulfil our redemptive purpose in our friend's life. The story of Pilgrim's Progress provides a useful picture of this. At different times on his journey the pilgrim is briefly assisted by *Evangelist, Faithful, Help, Watchful, Hopeful, The Interpreter* and many others. It is these 'right time, right place' redemptive relationships that make it possible for *Christian* to complete his pilgrimage. How is it that they turn up at just the right time? It is God at work. In His providence He sends true friends across the pilgrim's path whose words and actions create 'crossroads moments' that help the pilgrim make good choices.

Week 3 - Mission

Lifelong friendship and companionship is a beautiful gift, but it can only be given to very few. Nevertheless, we are called to be generous givers of friendship in the moment. Jesus illustrates loving our neighbour as ourselves by telling the story of two people whose lives cross only briefly, but in which the Samaritan is the best possible friend to the injured man when he is most needed (Luke 10:25-37).

Secondly, we should be concerned about wrapping other, more local relationships around our friend. We should be praying that God will bring other Christians into their life. We should be seeking out a local church family who will want to reach out to and love our friend. Then we will not lose our capacity to support our church family's relationships in the place where we have been planted.

Reflect

1. **Why is it important that we keep God in the centre of the redemptive story, rather than make ourselves responsible?**

___

2. **Why is it important that your friend discover a network of Christian relationships more than just you?**

___

Prayer:

Dear Lord, rather than being concerned about how much time and commitment another relationship in my life will take, help me to play my part in the redemptive journey of someone else and be a generous giver of friendship in the moment. Please take the strengths and giftings that You gave me and weave me into Your story of redemption for them today. Amen.

Week 3 - Mission

Survey 3

This survey will help inform your church leadership as they consider how best to support the vision of church as redemptive family. Cut out this page and return it to church. Your church leadership will provide ongoing feedback through the course of the series.

1. **What redemptive relationship(s) brought you to us?**

   _____
   _____
   _____
   _____
   _____
   _____
   _____

2. **What can we do to support you in your mission of nurturing redemptive relationships?**

   _____
   _____
   _____
   _____
   _____
   _____
   _____
   _____

3. **How can we release you to nurture redemptive relationships?**

   _____
   _____
   _____
   _____

Week 3 - Mission

4. What else have you been prompted about this week?

Week 4

WE ARE A FAMILY IN A PLACE ON A MISSION TOGETHER

"IMAGINE A CHURCH FAMILY WHERE EVERYONE IS LIVING FOR OTHERS. UNSUPPORTED CHRIST-FOLLOWERS ARE SUSCEPTIBLE TO BURNOUT AND FATIGUE, YET JESUS TELLS US THAT WHEN WE COME TO HIM WE WILL FIND HIS YOKE IS EASY AND HIS BURDEN LIGHT. YOUR CHURCH FAMILY AS THE SPIRIT-FILLED BODY OF CHRIST WANTS TO SHARE YOUR YOKE AND LIGHTEN YOUR BURDEN – WITHOUT TAKING AWAY YOUR OWN PERSONAL ROLE AND PURPOSE."

Week 4

WHAT WE MEAN BY...

Parish

The word 'parish' means an area served or cared for by the local church. There have been times when the concept has been used to extract payment from people or as a means of 'protecting turf' – keeping people out or in. Despite the baggage, we think there is too much value in the idea of parish for us to discard it.

At its heart, 'parish' is a redemptive way of seeing place. It is local church seeking the welfare of the place in which it is planted. It is church creating an open space within the community where everyone is welcome and can freely belong and where spiritual conversations can happen without being taboo. Central to the community's experience of parish is a core of people who know and love Jesus and who live out the gospel so that others may belong and come to believe.

Jesus used the analogy of yeast working through a lump of dough to describe how the kingdom grows. Both the yeast and the dough are important. 'Parish' is neither the church (the yeast) nor the community (the dough) but the interplay between them in a particular place.

To practise parish is therefore to stand shoulder-to-shoulder in solidarity with both our church family and with our community, taking every opportunity to build redemptive relationships.

Week 4 – Together

Day 1 – Doing Mission Together as Family

Read: Matthew 16:21-27

In today's Scripture reading Jesus tells us that whoever tries to hang on to their life to spend it selfishly will lose it, but anyone who gives up their life for His sake will save it (Matt. 16:25). We cannot selfishly hoard our time to spend on just ourselves. Our happiness and our personal and spiritual growth are paradoxically tied to us forgetting about ourselves and serving God and others.

Now imagine a church family where everyone is living for others. God placed us in families of Christ-followers to be an encouragement and support to each other as we each choose to live sacrificially. Unsupported Christ-followers are susceptible to burnout and fatigue, yet Jesus tells us that when we come to Him we will find His yoke is easy to bear and the burden He gives is light (Matt. 11:29-30). Your church family as the Spirit-filled body of Christ wants to share your yoke and lighten your burden – without taking away your own personal role and purpose.

Jesus said that all the law and the prophets could be summed up in two love relationships; loving the Lord our God with all our heart, soul, mind and strength and loving our neighbour as ourselves (Mark 12:30-31). These twin strands of DNA are inseparable and go to the heart of our church family's purpose. We cannot love God without loving our neighbour and we cannot truly love our neighbour without loving God first. We cannot separate worship and mission – they go hand in hand.

So what does being missioners together as a church family look like? Here are some reflections:

We share a clear picture of our pathway to success. We all seek to befriend others in our world and draw them closer to Jesus; through personal engagement, through wrapping other Christian relationships around them and then by inviting them to experience the church family for themselves.

Week 4 – Together

There is mutual accountability to all be missioners together. We take each other's hands to get the job done. You can ask your church friendship cluster to keep you accountable for building redemptive relationships in your world. They will ask how things are going, give you advice, pray for you regularly and help you find the resources you need. And you can do the same for them!

Mentoring and discipleship has a real world context. We will all grow in faith and maturity because we need God's help in our mission. When we as a church family are praying, wrestling with the questions posed by our new friends and discovering each other's gifts and wisdom in embracing those friends, we are being mentored and discipled better than in any classroom.

Church is an authentic experience of kingdom for newcomers. We want our new friends to experience the family table, believing that the church family gathered together is an authentic witness to the reality and power of God.

We will be exploring the benefits of sharing our redemptive relationships with our church family and the many ways we can do so in the week ahead.

Reflect

1. How do I feel about being part of a church family that expects me to be generous with my time?

   _____
   _____
   _____

2. Who in my friendship circle could I ask to keep me accountable as a missioner?

   _____
   _____

Prayer:

Dear Lord, there are times I take the comfort of being in Your presence and worshipping You and avoid the discomfort of reaching out to the lost ones You also love. Help me to truly worship and obey You by caring about what You care about. Forgive me for the times I have done less than I could have because I found it inconvenient. Please help me to joyfully share in a church family culture of living for others. Amen.

Week 4 – Together

Day 2 – Bringing My Two Worlds Together

Read: Luke 19:1-10

Jesus used meals as a way to have spiritual conversations and to forge redemptive relationships with people. Today's reading is one such example – Jesus spots Zacchaeus the tax-collector up a tree and bids him come down to take Jesus home for a meal with his family. The conversation goes so well that Zacchaeus experiences a saving change of heart. He spontaneously stands up in the middle of the meal to declare that he will give to the poor and recompense any whom he might have robbed.

Jesus has a similar meal with Levi in Mark 2:13-17. Jesus has already called Levi to follow him as a disciple and now he eats at Levi's house, surrounded by Levi's old friends and fellow tax collectors. What a lovely, congenial way to be introduced to Jesus, the soul-doctor. The Pharisees thought that mixing 'spiritual' and 'unspiritual' people together was a bad idea, but Jesus disagrees.

Invitation and hospitality are the simplest and most human way for me to include a friendship cluster from my church family in the redemptive journey of my new friend. In fact, a lot of good things happen when I bring my not-yet-Christian friends and my church family together.

My new friend benefits from meeting my Christian friends. I introduce them to a whole new network of friends who will be actively taking an interest in them. These new friends all love Jesus and so I am multiplying the number of spiritual conversations my new friend is going to have in the future. What is more, each of my Christian friends brings to this new relationship certain giftings, experience and wisdom that will enrich my new friend beyond what I alone am able to do. And let's not forget that as my new friend watches us together and sees our servant hearts, our openness and our humility, we are bearing witness to Jesus in ways that go beyond words.

My Christian friends benefit from meeting my not-yet-Christian friend. Being at the coalface of mission grows our faith and our dependence on God. It is also the best way to stay tuned to the culture around us and to not live in a bubble. It gives us all the opportunity to share in the good works that God prepared for

Week 4 - Together

us to do and to exercise our spiritual gifts, which shapes our own destiny and purpose; and for all involved it is also on-the-ground training in discipleship.

Doing stuff together shares the load and helps us get to know each other at a deeper level. When I feel sole responsibility for relationships I feel overburdened. By sharing my new relationships with others and only being responsible for being present in the moment I can engage with more people without burnout. It is also true that by working together we forge deeper bonds with each other. We discover new things about each other along the way that open up levels of understanding and compassion for each other that would not have happened otherwise.

As you begin thinking about the people you would like to be on mission with, consider that you don't all have to be peers of the same age and stage. Include some older heads for wisdom and some younger ones too so that the vision is shared with the next generation.

Reflect

1. Do I have a friendship circle within my church family that I would like to be on mission with?

_____
_____
_____
_____

2. Who in my two worlds could I bring together through invitation and hospitality?

_____
_____
_____
_____

Prayer:

Dear Lord, I long to play my part in growing Your kingdom. Open my eyes to the possibilities of how I could use hospitality in Your service. As I reach out to my Christian friends to join me in an everyday mission of friendship, may I find that their hearts have been captured by this dream also. May this band of brothers and sisters find simple ways to use food, drink and common interests as a means for many to taste the Kingdom. Amen.

Week 4 – Together

Day 3 – Serving Together in our Place

Read: Nehemiah 4

Yesterday we considered how we can share in growing the redemptive relationships we each initiate in our own world. Today we will be considering the relationships that will arise because of what we do together as a church family in our place.

Today's passage paints a striking picture of families working together shoulder-to-shoulder to rebuild the section of broken-down city wall in the place allocated to them. They rebuilt the wall despite the distractions of the enemy. They were prepared to endure the inconvenience of building with a sword in one hand in order to realise their vision of a better future for their city. Their labour was not only for their own sake but for all who lived there.

Similarly, our church families have been planted in a place to rebuild what the enemy has broken down. If we embrace parish we also labour not only for our own sake but for all who live there. This work is not easy; it has to be fitted in with jobs and families and other commitments. But the work is also not optional if we take our call to place and parish seriously.

As we saw in week 2, parish is a way of seeing place. Jesus used the analogy of yeast working through a lump of dough to describe how the kingdom grows. Both the yeast and the dough are important. The focus of parish is neither the church (the yeast) nor the community (the dough) but the interplay between them in a particular place. One day everyone on earth will acknowledge the reign of King Jesus and 'church' and 'community' will be one!

To practise parish is therefore to stand shoulder-to-shoulder in solidarity with both our church family and with our community. Working together shoulder-to-shoulder in our place creates many opportunities for building redemptive relationships.

You can do things together you could never do alone. If I knock on the door of someone down the road and ask if I can mow his lawn, I am likely to cause offence. However, if I tell him that a team is offering to mow the lawns of everyone in the neighbourhood, he is more likely to agree. Whether it's

Week 4 - Together

everyone in the neighbourhood, he is more likely to agree. Whether it's mowing lawns or throwing a party, the social dynamics of doing things as a group opens the door to a range of relationships none of us may have found on our own – and can be a lot of fun!

You can serve shoulder-to-shoulder with your neighbours. When you are serving a parish you literally share common ground with your neighbours. Their dreams for their place look like yours. They may not yet recognise the importance of embracing the King from whose hand every good gift comes, but that is why God planted your church family where He did. When you invite them to come alongside you to do something that will make their community a better place, many will join you – and spiritual conversations can begin!

The church need not only serve the community under its own banner. If our objective is to stand in solidarity with our place and to build redemptive relationships that draw folk to our family table, it doesn't matter if a good idea originated in the church or in the community. Our willingness to support community projects will increase community support for church projects too.

Reflect

1. *How do I experience the tension between the things I need to get done for myself and the call of my church to be involved in our community?*

___
___
___

2. *How is thinking 'parish' different to running community service activities?*

___
___
___

Prayer:

Dear Lord, there are things I like about my place and things I wish could change. Help me to see my place as you do, with all its potential for human thriving. Open our eyes to the opportunities you have given us as your church in this place to be conduits for blessing, healing, restoration and reconciliation where you have planted us. May we be so relentless in our pursuit of the good for our place that our community will want to stand shoulder-to-shoulder with us and us with them. Amen.

Week 4 - Together

Day 4 - The role of church programmes

Read: Acts 6:1-7

Through this devotional series we have been considering a simple model of missional church. At the heart of this model is the common mission of everyone in our church family to nurture and grow redemptive relationships that draw people closer to Jesus. This week we have been focusing on how we can take our mission to a different level through taking hands and growing redemptive relationships together. Yesterday we looked at working together, seeing our place through the eyes of parish; today we will consider the role of church programmes in our redemptive mission.

In today's passage we read about the first organised church programme. Making sure the widows within the church family were properly fed was so important in the early church context that it was initially handled by the apostles themselves. When they handed over responsibility for this function, it was to people 'full of the Spirit and wisdom'. The result is recorded in verse 7: 'So God's message continued to spread'. Here are some observations from this passage that undergird the role of church programmes in the model we have been reflecting on.

Church programmes serve the church family and are a beacon of hope to outsiders. How is it that feeding widows helped spread the word of God? One reason is that the church family was taking care of its own in ways that wider society was not. This is a concrete example of outsiders being able to look in and say, 'See how they love one another!' There are tangible benefits to belonging to the church family which are a powerful witness to those looking in. When they are invited to join us it is an invitation to experience all the benefits of salvation and family.

When programmes exist because the family needs them, the presence of church family within our programmes enriches relationships and spiritual conversations with the outsiders we invite. When programmes exist only for outsiders and do not involve the wider church family, relationship-building becomes the sole responsibility of the programme leaders.

Week 4 - Together

Church programmes aid the family mission of the church when they also support our redemptive relationships. While they serve the family, programmes provide opportunities for us to invite our friends to come and participate, knowing that whatever the programme is they will also hear and experience the gospel in action.

Church programmes are not a substitute for the personal mission of each family member. My faith will not grow and my love for God and my neighbour will not grow unless I am personally engaged in mission as God intended. When I choose to let others carry the burden of mission God intended for me, I grow weaker and they grow wearier – and through this dysfunction the body of Christ touches far fewer lives and can lose its way.

The church is not an entity somehow separate from its members that can be tasked with mission. Church as organisation can produce programmes, but church *as family* must provide the saving relationships at the heart of mission. We are the church and the mission is ours.

Reflect

1. What did you find most challenging about today's devotional?

_____
_____
_____

2. What has been your experience of church programmes as a place for relationship-building with outsiders?

_____
_____
_____

Prayer:

Dear Lord, there is so much potential within my church family to be a blessing to those both inside and outside the church. I pray that the act of serving and all the organisation needed for that will not cause us to forget why we are doing it in the first place – to glorify Jesus and to make Him known. I pray for the leaders of the programmes within my own church family, that they will not own sole responsibility for my church's mission. When I am tempted to leave to others the role you have purposed for me, may your Spirit gently remind me that everyone in the body must play their part. Amen.

Week 4 – Together

Day 5 – A place for others at the family table

Read: Revelation 22

What do we ultimately want for our new friends with whom we are building redemptive relationships? Our deepest desire is that they will enter into the fellowship of our church family and experience the same joy and purpose we have found in being united with Christ and with each other.

Today's passage describes the compelling future we want our friends to enjoy too. We will share life together in a city basking in God's *shalom*, beautiful and tranquil in every way, rich in healing and under the undisputed lordship of Jesus Christ. Not everyone will enter to enjoy this blissful state but it is our deep longing that they do. Verse 17 says: *'The Spirit and the bride say, "Come!" Let anyone who hears this say, "Come!" Let anyone who is thirsty come. Let anyone who desires drink freely from the water of life.'*

If the church family extends this invitation it must stand ready to welcome and include any soul-thirsty person at the family table. The family wants to grow and indeed must grow to fulfil its purpose. It is possible for church families to be friendly and yet form a closed circle against newcomers, choosing in the moment the comfort of those we already know over mission. We need to move beyond friendliness to embracing newcomers as friends.

So what do we mean by 'the family table'? It is evident from the New Testament that eating together was the norm for the early church and that what we call communion or the eucharist was originally observed in the context of a regular meal. It had social and ceremonial significance for the believers and was a hospitable connection point for seekers.

We can say that the family table is that part of our church family life together that captures the essential elements of table fellowship, whether we share an actual meal together or not. It is our best experience of church, one we want to share.

Week 4 – Together

It is where we experience:
- Being worshipfully alive to the presence of God with us, making us family
- Being welcomed and accepted without the need for pretence, even as a guest
- A place where we can share what we have with others and receive what we ourselves need
- A place of safety and trust, where important things can be discussed without fear
- A place where we can celebrate and grieve with each other
- An informal place where we can become known and learn to know others over time

Every church with a sense of family identity has 'family table' occasions. For every family these times are precious. We should strive to ensure that these times are protected and never become so structured as to lose their element of spontaneity. When outsiders arrive they need to experience a church family, not just a church service!

Over the past four weeks we have described an ideal, and no church family is perfect. However, where our eyes have been opened to new possibilities our church family can choose to grow and change. This is what we will be considering in our final week together.

Reflect

1. What is your best experience of church? What makes it special for you?

_____
_____
_____

2 How do you engage with visitors?

_____
_____
_____

Prayer:

Dear Lord, thank you for giving us the table to experience life together and to encourage each other. I long for us all to experience this more and more. Please open my eyes to the part I can play to enhance our experience of family and to make places at the table for others. Please help me to resist spending all my time with existing friends. For the times I have acted friendly towards a newcomer and then turned away and forgotten about them, please forgive me. May our informal family conversations be less about the trivial and the mundane and more centred on You and the things the really matter. Amen.

Week 4 – Together

Survey 4

This survey will help inform your church leadership as they consider how best to support the vision of church as redemptive family. Cut out this page and return it to church. Your church leadership will provide ongoing feedback through the course of the series.

1. **What has been your best experience of invitation and hospitality in the church context?**

   _____
   _____
   _____
   _____
   _____
   _____
   _____

2. **How would you describe our willingness to include outsiders in our church family?**

   _____
   _____
   _____
   _____
   _____
   _____
   _____

3. **How can the church use programmes and events to bring together insiders and outsiders?**

   _____
   _____
   _____

Week 4 - Together

4. What else have you been prompted about this week?

Week 5

WHAT YOU CAN DO

"YOU MUST TAKE THE FIRST STEP TOWARDS REALISING THIS VISION. IF EVERYONE WAITS FOR SOMEONE ELSE TO TAKE THE LEAD, CHANGE BECOMES IMPOSSIBLE. WE EACH NEED TO TAKE RESPONSIBILITY FOR OUR OWN LIFE, WHATEVER OTHERS MIGHT DO; AND IF ENOUGH OF US MAKE THE CHANGE, OTHERS WILL FOLLOW."

Week 5

WHAT WE MEAN BY...

Missioner

We usually attach and use labels to describe purpose. A toaster toasts; a conductor conducts; a doctor doctors the sick. You get the idea.

What shall we call ordinary church folk? Labels matter. 'Church-goers' or 'congregants' implies that our purpose is to go to church to congregate. 'Worshippers' implies our purpose is to worship. While this is important it does not get to the heart of the purpose of church: which is to glorify God in the world through the witness of our words, our deeds, our body life and the answers we receive to prayer. We need a label that reminds us that we are on a mission from God.

The label 'missionary' describes a purpose, but it is commonly understood in a specialist sense of one who takes the gospel across geographical and cultural borders. We would like to call ordinary church folk 'missioners'. It is an archaic word that used to just mean missionary, but as it has fallen out of our vocabulary why not recycle it and put it to good use?

WEEK 5 - WHAT YOU CAN DO

DAY 1 - DESIRE A DIFFERENT FUTURE

Read: Psalm 37:3-6

In today's scripture passage we learn that if we trust and delight in the Lord and determine to do what is right, He will help us dwell richly in our place and give us the desires of our heart. Is it the desire of your heart to be part of a church family that generously supports each other in mission for the sake of its parish, for the spiritual growth of its members and for the glory of God?

Over the past four weeks we have tried to capture your heart with a simple model of church consistent with Scripture that is centred in growing redemptive relationships together as a family.

In week 1 we saw that **for church, being family is central.** That we are family is supernatural evidence of God's grace. Holding hands we go out into the world to invite back seekers to experience this remarkable family for themselves.

In week 2 we acknowledged **our church family is in a place God intended.** Together we seek God's *shalom* for our place by embracing it and seeking to be present in it as God's reconciling agents.

In week 3 we discovered **our personal responsibility to grow redemptive relationships** in our place and the role of our church family to support us. A redemptive relationship is one in which I woo someone to Jesus through what I say, what I do and through answers to prayer.

In week 4 we considered the benefits of **introducing the friends we make in our personal world to our safe circle of Christian friends.** Together we may draw them to the church family table where they will be welcomed and discipled and can discover the life and role God intended for them.

You are journeying through this devotional material together as a church to bring new focus and clarity to what your church wants to be and do. Your church was founded on a vision, but just as we sometimes need to remodel our homes to cater for changing needs and circumstances, so it is with the church. God's purpose for His church has remained constant through the

Week 5 – What You Can Do

centuries, but our forms of church have changed with changing times. Your church's forms and practices can be reshaped to serve a fresh compelling vision in which everyone in church serves the mission of the church – and is growing spiritually as a result!

The 'redemptive family' model is simple and easy to understand, but its application is messy. For it to work we need to rely on each other as imperfect people for both accountability and support. At its heart it is all about relationships, which do not run to schedule and which can take unexpected turns. The timetable of such mission is largely in God's hands, not ours. The important question however, is not 'Will it be easy?' but, 'Is this what God wants from me?'

You have great influence! If you deeply desire a different future you will keep asking the questions that will lead to change.

It all begins with you. What is God's Spirit saying to you? If you have been stirred by this vision, don't let it pass you by simply because it can't be fulfilled by you alone. Determine today that, as far as it depends on you, you will be obedient to His calling.

Reflect

1. How could your church better embrace the 'redemptive family' model?

_____
_____
_____

2 What role could you play in your church to help bring this about?

_____
_____
_____

Prayer:

Dear Lord, I want to trust and delight in You above all else. Help me to also trust and delight in the gift from Your hand of enjoying safe pasture in the place You have planted me. Thank you for all the good things in my world and for the blessing of being part of my church family. Please align the desires of my heart with Your desires for how my place and my church family might intersect – and for the role You may want me play in that. Amen.

Week 5 - What You Can Do

Day 2 - Choose to lead yourself

Read: Ephesians 4:22-29

We have all heard the line 'insanity is doing the same thing and expecting a different outcome'. Needed change is something we embrace as Christians. Today's scripture tells us that we must keep taking off our old nature with its unworthy desires and keep putting on the new nature. In this perpetual process of change we gain a new attitude of mind and a new heart.

Yesterday we did a heart check. Is it the desire of your heart to be part of a church family that generously supports each other in mission for the sake of its parish, for the spiritual growth of its members and for the glory of God?

You must take the first step towards realising this vision. If everyone waits for someone else to take the lead, nothing will change. We each need to take responsibility for our own life, whatever others might do; and if enough of us make the change, others will follow.

What can you begin doing right now that will help shape your church in the direction of the vision we have described? Here are some suggestions:

Pray daily that God will open your eyes to opportunities. We have all missed opportunities to connect because we were not alive to what was happening in the moment. Proverbs 20:12 says, "Ears to hear and eyes to see – both are gifts from the Lord." Pray that God will open your eyes and ears to see and hear what those around you need.

Find a way to serve or bless somebody each day. No further explanation needed!

Safeguard a regular slot in your calendar for hospitality. If you really want to get to know someone, have them join you for a meal. Spontaneity has its place, but if you wait until you are less busy, hospitality may never happen. By scheduling in hospitality times and protecting them, there is less chance that busyness will rob you of something that is really important.

Week 5 – What You Can Do

Become a better conversationalist. The best conversationalists are those who are genuinely interested in the other person. Where possible, think about possible conversation topics ahead of time. Avoid questions that require only a 'yes' or 'no' answer. And be prepared to share appropriately about yourself – a conversation in which you only ask questions would be odd.

Become familiar with a gospel outline. If you are asked to explain your faith, it will be best if you can answer the question briefly and with clarity. Being clear about what the gospel is will not only help the other person, it will help your confidence too. Become familiar with a gospel outline recommended by your church, or find one you like online. You could even go through the rewarding exercise of writing your own!

Bring God glory and inspire others by telling the stories of what happened. One of the chief ways you will help shape your church is by telling the stories of your God-ordained encounters. Stories help make new behaviours normal and will help shift the culture of your church. A good story is a more powerful instrument for change than any textbook!

Reflect

1. **When have you chosen to lead yourself rather than run with the crowd?**
   _____
   _____
   _____

2. **Which of today's suggestions will you try first?**
   _____
   _____
   _____

Prayer:

Dear Lord, help me walk through my day in prayerful consciousness of You. Today I am on a mission from God! Open my eyes to the opportunities that will come my way to reach out to someone. Whether it be a conversation or just a moment to serve or bless somebody, help me to be ready with enough hope and faith to make the connection. Give me a story to tell that will encourage others to do the same! And then help me to do the same tomorrow. Amen.

Week 5 – What You Can Do

Day 3 – Find Others to Join You

Read: Ecclesiastes 4:12

Over the past two days we have focused on your personal commitment to making real the vision of your church as a redemptive family.

Being clear on the plan and summoning up the necessary willpower is not enough. Our mission requires that God do a supernatural work in our lives and the lives of others. There are also spiritual forces ranged against us that want us to fail. We need to rely not on our own strength but on the power of the Holy Spirit, submitting daily to the will and purposes of God.

But there is still one more thing that is within your power to do that will set the stage for your church becoming a mission-centred redemptive family.

As we saw in previous weeks, at the heart of the redemptive family model are circles of like-minded Christian friends who together befriend seekers and invite them to the family table. There is no need to wait. Why not reach out to three or four of your church friends who live nearby and explore forming a missional friendship circle right away? Forming a group will benefit each of you by providing mutual support, encouragement and accountability. As today's verse says, 'a triple-braided cord is not easily broken'.

The group does not have to be a peer group of people of the same age and stage of life. Including younger and older members can be refreshing! Who is in this group may also change over time – that is life. What will remain constant is the desire to be a support group for each other as you live a life of witness for Christ.

Here are some practical suggestions for what you can do together as a group:

Meet regularly. There is no need for the meeting to be long, but it helps if it is regular. Find a time that suits all of you and keep to it.

Keep the format regular too. Read some scripture; hear how everyone is going and the conversations they have had; offer advice where appropriate; ask how you can help; pray for each other and for the outsiders we are each wanting to reach.

Week 5 - What You Can Do

Prayerwalk together. It is important that our lives intersect with the place where God has planted our church family. A great way to allow God to soften our hearts and open our eyes to our place is to prayerwalk. This entails walking through your place, praying a blessing on those who live there, praying for the needs you see and the things God brings to your attention. Someone has said that prayerwalking is talking to God about our neighbours before we talk to our neighbours about God.

Host meals and do life with not-yet-Christian friends. Invitation and hospitality are our best means of growing relationships and having conversations that matter. By co-hosting meals or inviting others to join us in doing something together we create an event to which each of us can invite our seeking friends.

Reflect

1. *If you are going to be part of a missional friendship circle, is there something you have to lay down so that you have the time?*

_____
_____
_____
_____
_____

2. *Others in your church are also reading this today. Who do you wish would invite you to join their group? Why not call them instead?*

_____
_____
_____
_____
_____

Prayer:

Dear Lord, I long for a sense of purpose and belonging that makes living my life as witness for You not a burden but a delight. Please give me and my church friendship circle a compelling vision of what the future of our church could be: our church family growing with new arrivals, broken lives made whole, and harmony and reconciliation in our place! Help me to find and link arms with others from my church family who share this faith dream! Amen.

WEEK 5 - WHAT YOU CAN DO

DAY 4 - BE A GOOD INFLUENCE ON YOUR CHURCH FAMILY

Read: Hebrews 10:19-25

You don't have to be a leader to be influential. We all influence the people around us every day by who we are, by what we say and what we do.

If you put the past two days into practice, you will be leading yourself well and your example will already be influencing the church family for good. What more can you do to be a good influence on your church family? Today's passage instructs us to "think of ways to motivate one another on to acts of love and good works" (10:24). Here are some ways:

Be a champion of the vision. The model of church mission that we have called 'Redemptive Family' doesn't require special training or funding and can include everyone. How this is applied in your specific context will require the ideas and imagination of the whole family – and that includes you.

Some aspect of this model has fired your imagination over the past five weeks. If you can articulate the vision and become a champion of the part that excites you, you will be contributing to the big picture. Keep bringing the family conversation back to what is important. The questions you ask privately and in public forums will help take change in the desired direction.

Include others in your church family in what you do. Yesterday we suggested that you gather a small group of like-minded individuals around you for support and accountability as you personally pursue a redemptive lifestyle. Your support group can give others in your church family little tastes of what doing mission together might be like through one-off invitations to meals with outsiders, or joining you for a prayer walk of the neighbourhood. These experiences will open their eyes and hearts to possibilities they might not otherwise have considered.

A key way to include your church family in what you are doing is to **tell your stories.** Use the channels (e.g. social media) that already exist in your church. Make sure your leaders know about your story so that they can use it.

Week 5 - What You Can Do

Be a cheerleader for the good things your church is already doing. There are many things your church is already doing that serve the vision of redemptive family. These activities and aspects of church life need to be celebrated. The ways in which they can connect to and feed into a bigger vision need to be explored. Be both vocal and practical in your support, and help others see how these things can feed into the bigger vision.

Not everyone will immediately 'get it'. Some of us are excited by a new idea and want to run with it. Others need to see a working model before they can believe in it. Wherever folk are on the spectrum they need to be treated with kindness and respect. We need to carefully listen to everyone with fears and concerns to make sure they are understood. Through it all it is important that we remain positive and stay the course!

Reflect

1. *Think of a time when you were proud to be part of your church family. What made it good?*

_____
_____
_____
_____

2. *Is there a way you can share this memory with your church to encourage more stories like it?*

_____
_____
_____
_____

Prayer:

Dear Lord, help me to use my influence for good. I want to be a champion and a cheerleader for the things that make me proud to be in my church family. Help me to be encouraging of small beginnings. May I be generous with my time and my praise, and where it is within my power to include others in positive experiences of family please grant me the discernment to see it and the courage to do it. Amen.

Week 5 – What You Can Do

Day 5 – Be the best follower your leaders have ever seen

Read: 1 Kings 19:1-16

In today's passage we see the trajectory of a brave yet unsupported leader. Elijah, the leading prophet in Israel, has a crisis of faith and courage. Exhausted by his mighty faith-filled exploits and running on empty, he cries out to God in effect, "I am the only one left who cares!" When he discovers there are still 7,000 in Israel who share his passion and have not bowed to Baal, he is revived emotionally and spiritually. What a pity Elijah didn't know about those 7,000 who were on his side earlier!

Within the church family are those tasked with being leaders. Leadership is an important role, enabling the church family to better fulfil its mission. To successfully pursue our vision of church as redemptive family we need to remain in step with our leaders while still playing our part.

A good leader reminds us of our mission and helps create the structures and opportunities for the family to operate as it should.

A good follower personally owns the vision and leads themselves well in light of it. They are team players, using their giftings to help and encourage the family to succeed. They are not passive or hard to motivate, or waiting for others to take the initiative. Perhaps most importantly of all, they have an encouraging relationship with their leaders.

What specific practices will help you be a good follower who encourages your leaders? This is the sort of follower your leader will respect and want to hear from:

> A follower who **prays for their leaders** and seeks their best, never disparaging them to others and always choosing to believe the best about them.
>
> A follower who **listens to understand their leaders' point of view.** Your leaders must concern themselves with every aspect of church life and may consequently have a different perspective on the issues at hand. Hear them out before you confront them.

Week 5 - What You Can Do

A follower who **communicates commitment and encouragement**. Your leaders need feedback. They need to know that their contribution is being valued. When last did you tell your leaders that you appreciate them and that you back their vision for the church?

A follower who **demonstrates commitment** by rolling up their sleeves and getting stuck in. Putting your hand up to do some of the work (and getting it done) earns you respect.

A follower who **is not a lone ranger**. It is frustrating for leaders to have their plans disrupted by initiative-takers who didn't take the time to ask first. Taking initiative needs to be accompanied by good communication.

A follower who **persistently comes back to the vision**. Your leaders are human too. Just like Elijah they can lose focus and have their vision leak. They need encouraging and re-visioning like everyone else. Knowing that they are not the sole bearers of the vision will be a great relief to them!

Reflect

Congratulations! You have just completed a five week journey in which you have reflected on a model of church centred in growing redemptive relationships together as a family in the place where God has planted us.

How has the past five weeks changed the way you think about church and mission?

_____
_____
_____
_____
_____

Prayer:

Dear Lord, thank you for giving our church family the leaders we have. I pray you will grow them in faith and grace and guard them from attack by the Evil One. As our church enters on the journey of becoming a more mission-centred family, give our leaders courage to withstand the discouragement of pessimists and sceptics and the endurance to see it through. By Your grace may our church family grow to be ever more like what you intended for us to be. Amen.

Week 5—What You Can Do

Survey 5

This survey will help inform your church leadership as they consider how best to support the vision of church as redemptive family. Cut out this page and return it to church. Your church leadership will provide ongoing feedback through the course of the series.

1. What have you decided to do as a result of this devotional series?

_____
_____
_____
_____
_____
_____
_____

2. What can we do / what can we change to facilitate the new direction this family is taking?

_____
_____
_____
_____
_____
_____
_____

3. What else have you been prompted about this week?

_____
_____
_____
_____
_____

Small Group Studies

When used as part of the Redemptive Family church series, we suggest that these small group studies are done the week after the topic has been covered in the devotional and preached on the Sunday. This gives everyone time to reflect on the topic for themselves and it reinforces the Sunday message they have heard.

These small group studies use the well-known 'Serendipity' framework and will work in both new and established groups.

SMALL GROUP STUDY-1

Being Family

THE BIG IDEA: Being family is meant to be the everyday reality of every local church. Given our diversity, being authentic family is supernatural. It is a powerful witness to ourselves and to outsiders. To those who already belong, the family says 'your contribution is vital and we will share your load'. To those who are still on the outside looking in, the family holds out the promise that they can have their deep desire for both purpose and authentic community met here.

Open

1. What is your happiest childhood memory of being family together? How did this experience make you feel?

___

2. Have you ever been uncomfortable around someone because of their appearance or background yet later became friends? Tell of your experience.

___

Dig

Read: Romans 12:3-16

³ Because of the privilege and authority God has given me, I give each of you this warning: Don't think you are better than you really are. Be honest in your evaluation of yourselves, measuring yourselves by the faith God has given us.
⁴ Just as our bodies have many parts and each part has a special function,
⁵ so it is with Christ's body. We are many parts of one body, and we all belong

SMALL GROUP STUDY-1

to each other. **6** In his grace, God has given us different gifts for doing certain things well. So if God has given you the ability to prophesy, speak out with as much faith as God has given you. **7** If your gift is serving others, serve them well. If you are a teacher, teach well. **8** If your gift is to encourage others, be encouraging. If it is giving, give generously. If God has given you leadership ability, take the responsibility seriously. And if you have a gift for showing kindness to others, do it gladly. **9** Don't just pretend to love others. Really love them. Hate what is wrong. Hold tightly to what is good. **10** Love each other with genuine affection, and take delight in honoring each other.
11 Never be lazy, but work hard and serve the Lord enthusiastically. **12** Rejoice in our confident hope. Be patient in trouble, and keep on praying. **13** When God's people are in need, be ready to help them. Always be eager to practice hospitality. **14** Bless those who persecute you. Don't curse them; pray that God will bless them. **15** Be happy with those who are happy, and weep with those who weep. **16** Live in harmony with each other. Don't be too proud to enjoy the company of ordinary people. And don't think you know it all!

3. How does 'belonging to each other' (v. 5) run counter to our cultural conditioning?

_____
_____
_____
_____
_____

4. The passage mentions several ways we live out belonging to each other and supporting each other. How many can you find?

_____
_____
_____
_____
_____

SMALL GROUP STUDY-1

5. **In this passage Paul moves back and forth between talking about our conduct inside the family and our conduct outside it. How does consistently practising being authentic family together train us for mission together?**

___

6. **Imagine yourself an outsider looking in on a family living by these values. What would you be thinking and feeling?**

___

REFLECT

7. **What is our biggest challenge to putting this passage into practice for ourselves?**

___

8. **What is one thing this group can do to enrich our experience of family together?**

___

SMALL GROUP STUDY - 2

Embracing our place

THE BIG IDEA: God has a redemptive purpose for our church family being where it is. Even though we look forward to a 'new Jerusalem' God's plan for us is healthy rootedness in the place where He has planted us. Our faithful presence in our place makes transformational relationships possible.

Open

1. Are you more of a homebody or 'a rolling stone that gathers no moss'? How has this played out in your life?

   _____
   _____
   _____
   _____
   _____

2. Have you ever known someone who seemed to know everybody and always knew what was going on in the neighbourhood? What role did they play in the community?

   _____
   _____
   _____
   _____
   _____

Dig

Read: Jeremiah 29:4-14

[4] This is what the Lord of Heaven's Armies, the God of Israel, says to all the captives he has exiled to Babylon from Jerusalem: [5] "Build homes, and plan to stay. Plant gardens, and eat the food they produce. [6] Marry and have children. Then find spouses for them so that you may have many grandchildren. Multiply! Do not dwindle away! [7] And work for the peace and prosperity of the city where I sent you into exile. Pray to the Lord for it, for its welfare will determine your welfare." [8] This is what the Lord of Heaven's Armies, the God

SMALL GROUP STUDY-2

of Israel says: "Do not let your prophets and fortune-tellers who are with you in the land of Babylon trick you. Do not listen to their dreams, **9** because they are telling you lies in my name. I have not sent them," says the Lord. **10** This is what the Lord says: "You will be in Babylon for seventy years. But then I will come and do for you all the good things I have promised, and I will bring you home again. **11** For I know the plans I have for you," says the Lord. "They are plans for good and not for disaster, to give you a future and a hope. **12** In those days when you pray, I will listen. **13** If you look for me wholeheartedly, you will find me. **14** I will be found by you," says the Lord. "I will end your captivity and restore your fortunes. I will gather you out of the nations where I sent you and will bring you home again to your own land."

3. Look at 1 Peter 2:11-12. How is our situation as Christians similar to God's people in exile who are being addressed in this passage from Jeremiah?

_____
_____
_____
_____
_____

4. The false prophets spoken of in this passage were telling God's people not to settle down. Why do you think this was an appealing message to God's people in a foreign land?

_____
_____
_____
_____
_____

5. God had a purpose for His people putting down roots in Babylon. What reasons can you see from the passage?

_____
_____

SMALL GROUP STUDY - 2

6. God's message to those in exile was <u>not</u> that they should assimilate with the Babylonians by losing their identity or by giving up their religious practices or hope of future rescue. What impact do you imagine they had by both 'seeking the prosperity of the city' and being true to their God?

REFLECT

7. If we as a church family are taking our belonging to our place seriously, what difference can we expect to make?

8. What is one thing this group can do to better embrace the place where God has planted us?

SMALL GROUP STUDY - 3

Our Mission: to nurture redemptive relationships

THE BIG IDEA: How do I transform the relationships God has placed in my life into redemptive relationships? Wooing people closer to Jesus is being redemptive. This involves seeking God's best for our friends with the hope of drawing them into our church family circle where they can grow as disciples of Jesus. To do this we need to hold on to our church family with one hand and on to our not-yet-Christian friends with the other, and do what we can to draw them closer together.

Open

1. *Have you ever had someone take a real interest in you that was more than skin deep? How did this make you feel?*

_____
_____
_____
_____
_____

2. *Has your relationship with anyone changed the course of your life for the better? Tell your story.*

_____
_____
_____
_____
_____

Dig

Read: 2 Corinthians 5:16-21

[16] So we have stopped evaluating others from a human point of view. At one time we thought of Christ merely from a human point of view. How differently we know him now! [17] This means that anyone who belongs to Christ has become a new person. The old life is gone; a new life has begun! [18] And all of

SMALL GROUP STUDY - 3

this is a gift from God, who brought us back to himself through Christ. And God has given us this task of reconciling people to him. **19** For God was in Christ, reconciling the world to himself, no longer counting people's sins against them. And he gave us this wonderful message of reconciliation. **20** So we are Christ's ambassadors; God is making his appeal through us. We speak for Christ when we plead, "Come back to God!" **21** For God made Christ, who never sinned, to be the offering for our sin, so that we could be made right with God through Christ.

3. **Paul challenges us to not regard others from a worldly point of view. What is the problem with doing this?**

_____
_____
_____
_____
_____

4. **Paul says if we are in Christ we are a new creation! This is now core to us. What have you noticed yourself? What do our friends tell us they see?**

_____
_____
_____
_____
_____

5. **Paul uses the word "reconciliation" frequently in this passage, which is all about mending relationships. Should this be the core mission of the church, or is there something else?**

_____
_____
_____
_____
_____

SMALL GROUP STUDY-3

6. *If we are to serve as ambassadors for Christ, what would need to be true?*

REFLECT

7. *This passage is full of 'us' and 'we' rather than 'me'. Is that significant?*

8. *What is one thing this group can do to help us grow to be ambassadors for Christ?*

SMALL GROUP STUDY-4

DOING MISSION TOGETHER AS FAMILY

THE BIG IDEA: So far on this journey we've discovered that as Christians we're designed to be family, embracing the place where we are and fulfilling our mission of nurturing redemptive relationships with the people we know. Today we will see that God never intended our mission to be done alone.

OPEN

1. *Have you ever been in a team that worked together to achieve something special? How did that make you feel?*

_____
_____
_____
_____
_____

DIG

Read: Ephesians 4:1-16

Therefore I, a prisoner for serving the Lord, beg you to lead a life worthy of your calling, for you have been called by God. **2** Always be humble and gentle. Be patient with each other, making allowance for each other's faults because of your love. **3** Make every effort to keep yourselves united in the Spirit, binding yourselves together with peace. **4** For there is one body and one Spirit, just as you have been called to one glorious hope for the future. **5** There is one Lord, one faith, one baptism, **6** one God and Father of all, who is over all, in all, and living through all. **7** However, he has given each one of us a special gift[a] through the generosity of Christ. **8** That is why the Scriptures say, "When he ascended to the heights, he led a crowd of captives and gave gifts to his people." **9** Notice that it says "he ascended." This clearly means that Christ also descended to our lowly world. **10** And the same one who descended is the one who ascended higher than all the heavens, so that he might fill the entire universe with himself. **11** Now these are the gifts Christ gave to the church: the apostles, the prophets, the evangelists, and the pastors and teachers. **12** Their responsibility is to equip God's people to do his work and build up the church, the body of Christ. **13** This will continue until we all come to such

SMALL GROUP STUDY - 4

unity in our faith and knowledge of God's Son that we will be mature in the Lord, measuring up to the full and complete standard of Christ. **14** Then we will no longer be immature like children. We won't be tossed and blown about by every wind of new teaching. We will not be influenced when people try to trick us with lies so clever they sound like the truth. **15** Instead, we will speak the truth in love, growing in every way more and more like Christ, who is the head of his body, the church. **16** He makes the whole body fit together perfectly. As each part does its own special work, it helps the other parts grow, so that the whole body is healthy and growing and full of love.

2. Verse 1 exhorts us to lead a life worthy of our calling. What is our calling? What Scriptures can you think of that relate to our calling?

_____

3. Verses 2-7 are about nurturing and protecting the church family. How is this related to us fulfilling our calling?

_____

4. Verse 8 points out that God has given gifts to His people. What gifts are mentioned and what is their purpose according to verses 11-13? What is your God-ordained role in this church family?

_____

SMALL GROUP STUDY-4

5. What is described in verses 14-16 is a church family discipling each other. What aspects of discipleship can you see in these verses?

_____
_____
_____
_____
_____

6. Verse 16 sums up the passage by telling us that this is how the church grows. Are you experiencing the body growing spiritually and numerically? Can you see the part you are meant to play?

_____
_____
_____
_____
_____

REFLECT

7. When others say 'I can be a Christian without going to church', they are really saying that personal salvation is the important thing and being part of a church family is optional. How would you respond?

_____
_____
_____
_____
_____

8. How can we be accountable to each other about the part we are playing in the mission of our church family?

_____
_____
_____
_____
_____

SMALL GROUP STUDY-5

CHANGE BEGINS WITH ME

THE BIG IDEA: If there are things to be done or behaviour that needs to change for our church to fully embrace its role as a redemptive family, the change needs to begin somewhere. If everyone waits for someone else to take the lead, nothing will change. We each need to take responsibility for our own life, whatever others might do; and if enough of us make the change, others will follow.

OPEN

1. Have you ever given up something good in order to gain something better?

_____
_____
_____
_____
_____

DIG

Read: Hebrews 10:11-25

¹¹ Under the old covenant, the priest stands and ministers before the altar day after day, offering the same sacrifices again and again, which can never take away sins. ¹² But our High Priest offered himself to God as a single sacrifice for sins, good for all time. Then he sat down in the place of honor at God's right hand. ¹³ There he waits until his enemies are humbled and made a footstool under his feet. ¹⁴ For by that one offering he forever made perfect those who are being made holy. ¹⁵ And the Holy Spirit also testifies that this is so. For he says, ¹⁶ "This is the new covenant I will make with my people on that day, says the Lord: I will put my laws in their hearts, and I will write them on their minds." ¹⁷ Then he says, "I will never again remember their sins and lawless deeds." ¹⁸ And when sins have been forgiven, there is no need to offer any more sacrifices. ¹⁹ And so, dear brothers and sisters, we can boldly enter heaven's Most Holy Place because of the blood of Jesus. ²⁰ By his death, Jesus opened a new and life-giving way through the curtain into the Most Holy Place. ²¹ And since we have a great High Priest who rules over God's house,

SMALL GROUP STUDY-5

22 let us go right into the presence of God with sincere hearts fully trusting him. For our guilty consciences have been sprinkled with Christ's blood to make us clean, and our bodies have been washed with pure water. **23** Let us hold tightly without wavering to the hope we affirm, for God can be trusted to keep his promise. **24** Let us think of ways to motivate one another to acts of love and good works. **25** And let us not neglect our meeting together, as some people do, but encourage one another, especially now that the day of his return is drawing near.

2. **Verses 11-18 compares the Old Testament way of being in right relationship with God with the New Testament way. The writer to the Hebrews is addressing an audience uncomfortably torn between the old and the new. Why do you think this was so? Why was it important that they give up the old way?**

   _____
   _____
   _____
   _____
   _____

3. **As we have journeyed through the Redemptive Family series together some may have been envisioned or convicted by the Holy Spirit that change is necessary (v.15). What have you heard the Spirit say to you?**

   _____
   _____
   _____
   _____
   _____

4. **The next part of this passage (vv.19-23) emphasises our spiritual <u>independence</u>. Even though we are part of a church family we also have to stand on our own two feet spiritually and we each have direct personal access to God. In light of this, what is my responsibility if God has spoken to me over these past weeks?**

   _____
   _____

SMALL GROUP STUDY - 5

_____
_____
_____

5. The latter part of this passage (vv.24-25) emphasises our spiritual <u>interdependence</u>. Why is it not enough to seek to do God's will on my own? Why do we need to be spurring on and encouraging one another?

_____
_____
_____
_____
_____

6. The passage concludes with the <u>urgency</u> of our mission, because Jesus is coming back (v.25). How does this fact colour what we have been talking about?

_____
_____
_____
_____
_____

REFLECT

7. How can this group be a role-model for behaviour that will help our church embrace its role as a redemptive family?

_____
_____
_____
_____
_____

A WORD TO CHURCH LEADERS

So what next?

Having shown your church a peek of what it might look like to be a redemptive family, you will want to keep the conversation going so your church doesn't drift back into its old ways.

One of the most powerful ways to consolidate change is to have your people come to own the change for themselves. They need to imagine themselves behaving in concrete new ways - and really like what they see! They will then be ready to take first steps.

A great way to achieve this objective is by engaging your whole church in a conversation about the church they dream of being, and then together designing a pathway to make that dream a reality. Love Your Neighbour has the experience and expertise to help you run a church-wide workshop that will do just that.

We facilitate church-wide conversations

Love Your Neighbour has many years' experience in structuring and facilitating conversations for large groups, and leading workshops for whole churches is our speciality. Using the process of Appreciative Inquiry and including group conversation formats such as World Café and Open Space Technology we can help your church discover the future it most desires.

All we do is at the invitation of a host church and in consultation with your leadership.

Contact us today and let's have a conversation about how we can serve you!

Howard: howard@loveyourneighbour.nz
Bruce: bruce@loveyourneighbour.nz
www.loveyourneighbour.nz

Love Your Neighbour is a registered charitable trust based at
126 Point Chevalier Road, Point Chevalier, Auckland.

Torn Curtain Publishing
Wellington, New Zealand
www.torncurtainpublishing.com

© Copyright 2021 Howard Webb. All rights reserved.

ISBN Softcover 978-0-473-57001-9

No portion of this book may be reproduced, stored in a retrieval system or transmitted in any form or by any means—electronic, mechanical, photocopy, recording or otherwise—except for brief quotations in printed reviews of promotion, without prior written permission from the author.

All text in bold or in parentheses are the author's own.

Scripture quotations are taken from the Holy Bible, New Living Translation, copyright ©1996, 2004, 2015 by Tyndale House Foundation. Used by permission of Tyndale House Publishers, Carol Stream, Illinois 60188. All rights reserved.

Cataloguing in Publishing Data
Title: Redemptive Family Devotional & Workbook
Author: Howard Webb

A copy of this title is held at the National Library of New Zealand.